Developing Apostolic Strategy

8 Keys to Projecting Power into Every Sphere of Society

Commander Tim Taylor
USNR-ret

All scripture quotations, unless otherwise indicated, are from the *New King James Version* © 1982 by Thomas Nelson, Inc.

Developing Apostolic Strategy

8 Keys to Projecting Power into Every Sphere of Society

Kingdom League International

4004 NE 4th Street, Suite 107-350

Renton, WA 98056

CONTENTS

The Function of the Apostolic Gift Today

When Jesus ascended on high He gave gifts unto men. The first gift was that of the apostle. In the early church, the first mission of people with that gift was to lay foundation. As part of laying the foundation, several of the early apostles wrote letters that formed the New Testament cannon of scripture. Some believe that once the scriptures were written the work of the apostolic gift was complete. I don't believe that is true. The cannon of scripture is complete, but the work of building His Church and expanding His kingdom is not. Building and expanding the kingdom is another part of laying foundation. Isaiah 9:7 says "of the increase of His government there will be no end," indicating that this is an ongoing work.

A study of the characteristics of the apostolic gift makes it easy to identify how various people with this gift function in building and expanding the kingdom today. God's government establishes order and justice where ever it goes. This is a foundational pioneering work which requires the functioning of an apostolic gift. Those with this gift lay foundations always in reference to Jesus Christ, the Chief Cornerstone.

We will be richly blessed if we recognize and receive the functioning of this gift because the apostolic gift was given to us, the Church, for our benefit. It is my conviction that God has deposited people with this gift in many cities and regions today. Those who operate it are key to discovering God's strategy to transform their respective areas. It is my hope and sincere prayer that we will begin to discover, recognize and receive those who carry these wonderful gifts given by Jesus to His bride.

The History of the Word and Work of the Apostle

This chapter is intended to focus on a strategic facet of the apostolic gift that I believe is often overlooked. It is not intended to be a complete study. Let us begin with Ephesians 4:11. Here, five gifts are listed. Some refer to these as the fivefold ministry because five are mentioned: apostle, prophet, evangelist, pastor and teacher. Prophet, evangelist and teacher were common religious terms in Hebrew culture. Pastor, or shepherd, was a familiar agricultural term. However, apostle was not a word from the Hebrew culture.

The word apostle was first a Greek/Phoenician seafaring term that meant leader of a convoy of ships. Later it came to refer to the commander of an invasion force. As time went on the Romans used it to refer to former generals who then became ambassadors. The Jewish culture eventually began to use it when speaking of an envoy who collected tribute. Finally, Jesus used it speaking of the first 12 disciples. In summary the history of the word meant:

- The leader of a convoy of ships
- The commander of an invasion force
- An ambassador general sent to represent a government to another nation

I have often said that the Lord used the Navy as a seminary for me. I spent my early years in the Navy as a training officer in a convoy unit. Convoy units only existed in the reserve and were called into service when war demanded it. Hence, I was recalled to serve in Desert Storm because of the demand for convoy operations. While serving in the Gulf War, I spent half of my time on the staff of Rear Admiral Taylor (no relation) as his expert on convoy operations and as a watch officer. I also had the privilege of working out of an embassy for six weeks. Admiral Taylor oversaw naval operations and was the commander of an invasion force. The Lord provided me an illustrated lesson through this experience which gave me greater understanding of His position as the Lord of Hosts.

Later I attended the Navy War College and studied the principles of war. As I spent time in God's word and in prayer, He taught me about the gift and role of an apostle through the eyes of a commander versus through the eyes of a pastor. This kind of training is not available in any seminary.

> *2 Corinthians 10:3-4 For though we walk in the flesh, we do not war according to the flesh. For the weapons of our warfare are not carnal but mighty in God for pulling down strongholds...*

The word "war" in the Greek means to serve in a military campaign and to "execute the apostolate." Apostolate literally means the office of apostle. The word warfare in the Greek means "apostolic career" or "strategy." Hence, one of the primary functions of the apostolic gift is spiritual warfare. God made people with this gift to develop strategy.

One of the major characteristics of people with this gift is that they hold an anointing for organizing, mobilizing, and developing strategy, like an admiral or a general does. Admirals or generals must think beyond one ship or one unit. They think about the bigger picture, which includes many ships and many units. They also think about how they need to work together in order to achieve a common objective. In the church, those with apostolic gifts work with a much broader, longer range perspective because of the assignments God gives them. They work with many local congregations and are responsible to help them function as a team to expand the kingdom and build our Lord's Church.

> *The apostolic gift is anointed to create strategy for spiritual war*

For example, in 2009 I worked with several apostolic leaders in 108 cities who mobilized 6,000+ churches in Operation Rolling Thunder. Each congregation required one or more pastor, depending upon their size. Similarly, each city requires one or more people with apostolic gifts to develop the teamwork and strategy to transform that city through the presentation of the gospel of the kingdom of our Lord Jesus Christ.

What is the most common ministry gift we see today? It is the pastor. This should be the most common gift. The shepherd is made to work with a specific number of sheep; sheep that the shepherd knows by name. Hence there is a limit to the number of people that a pastor can effectively oversee. The word pastor is only used once in the New Testament in the context of functioning in the Church (Ephesians 4:11). However, the word apostle is used 79 times in the New Testament, and prophets are mentioned over 150 times.

Why is it that the gift mentioned the least is today spoken of the most? I've already highlighted one reason – because we need many pastors to take care of the people. Another reason, I believe, is that while every ministry gift has a unique function and purpose, the apostle, prophet, evangelist and teacher should at their cores have pastor's hearts for God's people.

In many traditions, due to custom or a fear of pride they choose to call every minister a pastor. I understand that traditions differ. However, we often need to make distinctions based on function. For example, a carpenter carries tools with him to the job. He has a saw, a hammer, a common screw driver, a Phillips screw driver, a tape measure, a level and more. Suppose a carpenter needed to use a sheet rock screw to attach a fixture. If he yelled to his helper by the truck, "Hey, bring me a tool," would that helper know which tool to bring? No! Who knows what he would bring to the carpenter? The carpenter would tell his helper which specific tool he needed. Calling every minister a pastor is like calling every implement a tool. One of the reasons we have seen so little transformation in many cities where true pastors are at the helm is that God did not design the pastoral gift for strategy. He designed the apostle and prophet for that.

Apostles and prophets serve specific functions in the church. This is one reason that I believe the gifts of apostle and prophet are mentioned most often in the New Testament. The second is that the Church was at the beginning stage in its development, so it needed broad leadership.

The functional order of these gifts is detailed in 1 Corinthians 12:28. God made the apostolic gift to be utilized first and the prophetic to be second. God designed these two gifts for spiritual war, strategy and for building on a large scale. Whether the goal is to plant a church or to transform a city, the apostle and prophet act as catalysts. As catalysts they stimulate and facilitate the other giftings in their respective roles to build the kingdom.

DIFFERENT PERSPECTIVES OF THE PASTORAL AND APOSTOLIC GIFTS

Bible schools and seminaries today train leaders how to "pastor." We need many pastors because God designed them to be with people; to oversee, tend, nurture and protect a flock. I don't know of any schools or seminaries that teach how to "apostle." If there were, leaders would have a much better understanding of strategy. God trained me for strategy and war (the apostolic gift) all through my naval career. It is truly remarkable how closely my naval career modeled the etymology of the word apostle.

This perspective does not make the apostolic gift more important than the pastoral gift. It makes it different because of its function. For many years I have believed that the most important gift was the gift needed in a specific situation at a specific time. Depending upon the situation, each of the gifts – fivefold gifts, Romans 12 gifts, or 1 Corinthians 12 gifts – could be the most important gift. For instance, if a family needs counseling, then their local pastor is probably best suited for this task. But, to discover God's best solution for strategic situations, it is best to consult with a variety of people who carry several different gifts. For example, if several local congregations need a strategy to transform a city, then someone with an apostolic gift working with prophets would be best. This is when someone with the apostolic gift, which excels at teamwork, can help those with a variety of other gifts to function together.

HIERARCHY VERSUS FUNCTION

1 Corinthians 12:28-31 And God has appointed these in the church: first apostles, second prophets, third teachers, after that miracles, then gifts of healings, helps, administrations, varieties of tongues. Are all apostles? Are all prophets? Are all teachers? Are all workers of miracles? Do all have gifts of healings? Do all speak with tongues? Do all interpret? But earnestly desire the best* gifts. And yet I show you a more excellent way.

The scripture above is powerful. It is not describing an order of hierarchy but an order of function. There are two gifts made to develop strategy for spiritual war: apostles and prophets.[i] Both of these gifts operate with revelation. The apostolic gift also has a gift of wisdom, which is needed for building[ii] and for war.[iii] To build you need blue prints, or a plan, for the work. Apostles receive these strategic plans by revelation. A New Testament example is shown in 1 Corinthians 3:10 where the apostle Paul was described as being anointed as a "wise master builder" or spiritual architect.

Traditionally, the apostolic gift has been viewed as being used for planting churches or opening up unreached nations to the gospel. These are valid functions of the gift. But I want to submit that this gift is needed whenever or wherever God wants to birth something new, whether that is a new work or a new strategy. It is important for us to be able to identify this gift for strategy in people today. Jesus taught that if you want to receive the benefit of a gift, you have to recognize that gift.[iv]

As an example, I'll share a portion of my life. My call is not so much to a territory but to a function. It is to connect a body so that it can be raised up as an exceedingly great and mighty army, as spoken of in Ezekiel 37 and Joel 2. My mission includes helping to build our Father's house of prayer for all nations[v] in the spirit of the restoration of David's tabernacle.[vi] Operation Rolling Thunder and CONECT are strategic expressions of my apostolic gift at work. The fruit of my gift has been expressed by:

- **Revelation** – I have prepared by revelation for this season since 1993.[vii] God shared His dream with me for a new strategy that lays the foundation in cities to connect the strategic leaders at the gates of a city, connect the Body of Christ, and mobilize it as an army while building His house of prayer for all nations in the spirit of the restoration of David's tabernacle.
- **Spiritual Architect and Catalyst** – God gave me by the spirit the plans for CONECT in 1993. CONECT has affected cities and has established prayer ministries in churches, transforming previously unsuccessful efforts into successful programs. In December 2004 God gave me the plans for Operation Rolling Thunder (ORT). ORT started as a word. Within 5 months it spread to 80+ churches in 10 cities doing 10 days of twenty four seven (24/7) prayer. Within 4 years it grew to over 6,000 churches, in 107 cities, and 13 states in 24 nations.

  - The ORT apostolic plan, when followed, helps identify, connect and honor local leaders, empowering them to develop strategies appropriate for their territories, to build networks, and to connect networks, while capturing a strategic opportunity to affect their local community in the midst of national and international prayer events.
  - ORT provides a way to pray globally while connecting locally. It sets people up to successfully transform their communities.
- **Bringing Order and Government** – CONECTers in nations, states, counties, cities and churches have been raised up to connect the Body of Christ, each in their assigned territories, for 24/7 prayer while forming and or supporting apostolic councils representing all seven spheres of society. One of the evidences of a governmental church is that its prayers affect crime rates in its city.[viii]
- **Working with Five Fold Gifts** – Through the formation of Transformation Task Forces, we discover and include many people who carry other gifts described in Ephesians 4, Romans 12 and 1 Corinthians 12. While we need all the gifts, we pay particular attention to identifying and honoring those

with apostolic and prophetic gifts, as they are key to determining each area of geography's specific strategy.[ix]

- **Ambassador with Supernatural Signs and Wonders and Measurable Results Following** – Unusual signs and wonders have followed me since I began presenting my message. We've found that when God's people respond and/or when other CONECTers present the same message, similar signs and wonders follow them. Such signs include solar storms, thunderstorms, thunder-snow, rainbows, record rainfall, broken droughts, decreased crime, earthquakes, increased salvations, reconciliation with First Nations, increased healings, water baptisms and much more.[x]

- **Anointed for Strategy and Spiritual War** – Since 1993 I have been teaching leaders about the apostolic principles of corporate spiritual warfare. Now, leaders who are applying the Biblical principles and strategies contained within ORT and CONECT are equipped to develop their own apostolic strategies. The fruit has contributed to the shutting down of abortion clinics, decreasing crime, breaking droughts, reaping record harvests, healings, salvations and much more. The Church has been equipped to mobilize and project power at strategic targets. The results of ORT and CONECT speak for themselves.[xi]

- **Authority** – God has given me authority and an anointing to connect the Body of Christ, establish 24/7 prayer, and train leaders to think, act, plan and pray as admirals or generals. My understanding of geographic boundaries and spheres of authority enables me to mobilize and connect the Body of Christ like a military unit and then turn the unit over to local leaders. In some ways this is similar to what Paul instructed Titus to do. It establishes order which sets the church up to exercise her authority within a region.[xii]

I have just given you an example of this gift working through me in the context of prayer mobilization and city/regional transformation. I have also applied this successfully in other areas such as during Desert Storm. It helped me develop new processes and systems which led to rewriting 40 year old NATO doctrine. The gift and principles also worked in the corporate world where I trained leaders to develop rollout strategies. The largest rollout mobilized 40,000 employees spread across five countries in four months. It guided teams that developed new curriculum, new departments, and remedied organizational problems in various divisions. I took one department from conceptualization to foundation. The team in this initiative processed a half a billion dollars in transactions over six months with no errors. The business world did not call my gift apostolic. They called my skill set "strategic planner" or "change management expert."

RECOGNIZING APOSTOLIC WORK IN OTHERS

One of the reasons I have shared this portion of my life is to highlight some of the characteristics of an apostolic gift that God is using to mobilize and connect the Body of Christ in regions around the world. This is not the work with which the apostolic gift is traditionally associated. This work requires the strategy of a general, the design of an architect, and the heart of a father to birth a strategy that unites and mobilizes the church to effect transformation in many nations. The strategy began with a prophetic word in December 2004 and spread to over 108 cities and 6,000 churches in 24 nations in 2009. It equipped leaders to unite the church, from Catholic to Charismatic and from Presbyterian to Pentecostal. It empowered these churches to project power to transform their communities in a new way. The message and the strategies have been marked by signs, wonders and measurable results.

My Objective: Equip you to think, plan and pray strategically like an admiral, a general or an apostle.

There are other people with apostolic gifts who are performing similar functions on different assignments. Sometimes people recognize those with this type of apostolic gift, but much of the time they do not. It is my hope that you'll begin to recognize the characteristics of this particular strategic gift. We need these people. I thank God for them. If we recognize them we can be blessed by them.

1 Peter 2:17 Honor all people. Love the brotherhood. Fear God. Honor the king.

I celebrate the gifts God put within each of you. I want to see every one of you completely fulfill your destiny in Christ. Ephesians 4:16 teaches that it actually hurts me if you do not fulfill your destiny. Therefore, I am praying that each of you fulfill your destiny.

I encourage you to honor and celebrate the people with strategic apostolic gifts whom God has placed in each one of the seven spheres of society. I believe God has placed people with apostolic gifts in every nation, province, state, and city. The people so gifted carry strategic insight into what it will take to transform their areas for the glory of our Lord Jesus Christ. Further, I encourage you to be willing to recognize the gift in your own life. If you have it, the gift is not yours; it belongs to the Body of Christ. I pray that God will give you wisdom about how to steward the gift He placed in your life for us.

I have emphasized the strategic aspect of the gift of apostle. There are many who have the gift, but who are not recognized locally. **We need to see those who have these gifts be recognized and honored so that we can glean the benefit of the wisdom and strategy they can bring to help transform a city.** This is important because as taught in 1 Corinthians 12:28, the apostolic is the first gift that needs to function strategically. It sets all the other gifts that follow to build upon the foundation so that the Body might be strong and healthy. The church, business, government, media, education, healthcare and the family all require strategies to spread the gospel of the kingdom.

It is my hope that this book will help you to identify strategic leaders as well as equip you to develop strategy. The apostolic gift is key to providing a foundation for others to build upon. We need EVERY GIFT functioning and we need EVERY PERSON connected in the body as it pleases our Father. I pray that you find your place, that your gift is honored and that you begin to function in all fullness through the anointing of the Holy Spirit and the love of the Father.

Projecting Power into Every Sphere

One of the chief characteristics of the apostolic gift is that it is designed to develop strategy for spiritual war. Why is this significant? First, the Church is likened to an army that is in a war.[xiii] Second, the most prominent of the Jehovah names is Jehovah Tsaba (Yahweh Sabaoth),[xiv] the Lord of Hosts, or Lord of the Armies.

Think about this: a revelation of God's name reveals a portion of His character. This revelation is accompanied by an understanding of the covenant provision God has made for His people. I often ask my audience, "How many of you have been blessed by a revelation of God's name as Jehovah Jireh, the Lord My Provider?"[xv] Often 90% of the room raises their hands. Then I ask, "How many of you have been affected and blessed by a revelation of God's name as the Lord My Healer; Jehovah Rapha?"[xvi] Often the same group raises their hands. Then I ask, "How many times is Jehovah Rapha or Jehovah Jireh mentioned in scripture?" The answer is only one time.

We know that God is the author of the Bible. If an author is trying to make a point, does he emphasize something more often or less often? He emphasizes it more often. Jehovah Tsaba, the Lord of Hosts, is mentioned over 245 times in scripture. That is about 2.5 times more than any of the other Jehovah names.

Armies exist to project power to enforce the will of their government.

The army of the Lord is emphasized in scripture. It exists to project power to enforce the will of King Jesus, who taught us to pray "thy kingdom come and thy will be done on earth as it is in heaven." I learned in the Navy War College that armies exist to project power to enforce the will of their government. The purpose of the Church is to project power so that heaven is manifested on earth.

THE LEADERSHIP FACTOR

Leadership, or the lack thereof, affects the amount of power available to be projected. Although the principle of mass, which defines combat power, is one of the factors that determine power, in the hands of an unskilled leader even a very large force will have reduced power. A small force in the hands of a skillful leader is often more powerful and effective. There are several variables that affect mass, which we will look at later. For now, I want to focus on leadership.

> *The purpose of the Church is to project power so that heaven is manifested on earth.*

Leadership is a Biblical concept. Let me explain. I was privileged in my naval career to have the opportunity to attend a strategy course at the Naval War College. I studied the major strategies and principles that have been taught to professional military officers for over 2,500 years. They are taught because they work. We learned that the principles, or strategies, never change; only weapons have change. Therefore we could study ancient battles, learn from them and even apply their principles today. I learned that there are eight major principles. As we began to study these principles I had an epiphany. Every principle I was being taught had a Biblical basis. No wonder these timeless principles worked! When I recognized that our God is called Lord of the Hosts more than 2.5 times more than any of the other Jehovah names, then I understood who the real author of strategy is. Our Lord is the author of strategy.

Biblical principles of strategy are like the laws of gravity and aerodynamics. If one applies the law of aerodynamics properly, they can overcome the law of gravity for a period of time. Just as these laws work for anyone when applied properly, so do the timeless principles of strategy. It does not matter if you are a Christian or not. These laws work for anyone who applies them.

The apostle and prophet are two Biblical giftings that God designed to apply these principles for war and for building.[xvii]

> *2 Corinthians 10:3-4 For though we walk in the flesh, we do not war according to the flesh. For the weapons of our warfare are not carnal but mighty in God for pulling down strongholds...*

The word "war"[xviii] means "to execute the apostolate." Apostolate means the office of apostle. It also means to serve in a military campaign. The word translated warfare[xix] is where we get the word for strategy. It means apostolic career.

In Jeremiah 1:5-10 we discover that the prophetic gift was made for war. The prophet was to root out, pull down, destroy and throw down. He was then to build and to plant. Remarkably, this order of function is described in the first principle of war which we'll look at later. We find in the New Testament that the apostle and prophet were designed to work together through revelation.[xx] While the revelatory gift of the prophet is important in gathering intelligence, the apostolic gift functions with revelation combined with a gift of wisdom. This pragmatic gift of wisdom plays a critical role in developing the strategy, or the blueprints, for war.

Objective 2: Equip you, as a leader, to do a better job of projecting power into all of the areas where you have responsibility

The Book of Proverbs is clear in stating that wisdom, knowledge and understanding can be acquired if they are sought. *The first purpose of this book is to equip you, the reader, with wisdom and a basic understanding of the eight major principles of war so that you can be a more skillful strategic leader.*

CALLED TO BE KINGS AND PRIESTS

The Book of Revelation says that we are called to be kings and priests.[xxi] The role of the priest is described in Hebrews 7:25, where we see Jesus interceding and presenting offerings. But Revelation 19:11 shows us the purpose of kings. Their job is to make decisions, to judge, and to make war. Again the purpose of the army is to project power to enforce the will of the government, or kingdom, they represent. The message that King Jesus wants to be enforced is the gospel of the kingdom[xxii] In Matthew 6:9-12, He taught us to pray, "Lord let thy kingdom come and thy will be done on earth as it is in heaven."

Our second purpose is to equip you so you are better prepared to project power into all the areas where you have responsibility. This is the role of a king. So where do you have responsibility and authority? In the 7 spheres of society!

7 Spheres of Society

There are seven spheres in every society: church/religion, business, government, media/arts/entertainment, education, health-care and the family. Whether you go to the Americas, the Middle-East, Europe, or Southeast Asia these spheres exist everywhere. Some teachers refer to these spheres as mountains. Describing these areas either as mountains or as spheres is simply highlighting different facets of the concept which, when combined, gives us a better picture of the whole. Jesus used this technique when describing the kingdom, using several parables to describe the same thing. Therefore, referring to these areas as mountains or spheres is interchangeable.

Love is the first key in projecting power in the kingdom. Love for God and then love for people.

You have power or authority in accordance with your responsibility in your sphere. It is important to understand that although power can destroy, it can also build. For example, love is a power. Love can be expressed through a kind word to a stranger; the affectionate embrace of a father hugging his child; sending financial aid to disaster victims; confronting a friend; correcting destructive behavior by speaking the truth in love, or taking care of a sick family member.

Money is another form of power. According to Ecclesiastes 7:12 money is a defense, as well.

Deuteronomy 8:18 And you shall remember the Lord your God, for it is He who gives you power to get wealth that He may establish His covenant which He swore to your fathers, as it is this day.

The word translated wealth here can mean much more than money. It can also be properly translated army, force or band of men.[xxiii] Money can buy an army, or can be an expression of love if sending financial aid.

How you project power depends upon two things: what sphere you are in and what your role is. Here are some examples of this concept in each sphere.

CHURCH – PROJECTS POWER

- Changing lives by proclaiming the gospel of the kingdom and making disciples
- Intercessory prayer, praise and worship
- Alms and outreaches

How do you project power within the Church? Your interaction and the amount of power you have to project within the church will be determined by your role. A minister, an elder, a deacon, a Sunday school teacher, a member or a visitor, each have different types and levels of power.

BUSINESS – PROJECTS POWER

- Create wealth
- Create jobs

How do you project power in business? It depends upon several factors. First, in what kind of business are you engaged? Is it retail, wholesale, real-estate, investments, aerospace, biotech, or software? Secondly, projecting power is related to your role. There are two major roles to consider. One role is defined by your responsibility at your place of work. Your responsibility determines how much power you have to create products and services. For example a CEO, COO, a VP, a sole proprietor, a manager, a plumber, a janitor, a software engineer, a sales representative each have differing levels of power. Another role is that of a consumer. A consumer projects power by where they choose to purchase products and services.

GOVERNMENT – PROJECTS POWER

- Protects citizens
- Provides services
- Manages national destiny

It is important to recognize that all the spheres overlap. Take for example the area of wealth. Government does not create wealth; it consumes wealth through taxes. Without business providing jobs and revenue which can be taxed, the government would have no provision to offer its services.

Projecting power in government also depends upon your role. A president, a senator, a representative, a governor, or a mayor, each have differing levels of power in creating policies and laws. An employee of a government agency might be involved in offering services. Members of the armed forces are involved in our defense.

Citizens can project power through:

- Voting
- Serving as a volunteer on a campaign
- Giving money to a campaign
- Communicating with elected officials
  - Phone calls, emails and writing letters

MEDIA/ARTS/ENTERTAINMENT – PROJECTS POWER

- Information distribution
  - TV, radio, newspapers, magazines
- Arts and entertainment
  - Influence culture and every other sphere
  - Influence values
  - Closely tied to business

Here, the ability to project power is dependent upon the region or segment of society your media reaches, as well as what your role is. Consumers and producers have different roles. Consumers project power based on the time they devote to this area, and the amount of money they spend here. If you are a producer, your ability to project power is dependent on your responsibility, whether you are an owner of a TV station, a news anchor, an editor of a magazine, an actor, a radio personality, an artist, an owner of an art gallery, or a dance instructor.

EDUCATION – PROJECTS POWER

- Influencing values and culture
- Providing productive skills
- Knowledge is power

Consider whether you are a student, an educator, or one who serves in a support role, such as administration. Teachers, principals, and those who develop curriculum all play important roles in delivering the information used to shape values and culture. Students project power by where they choose to spend their time and money. Poorly attended classes are eventually discontinued.

HEALTH-CARE – PROJECTS POWER

- Health increases the productivity of a society.

Doctors, nurses, x-ray technicians, chiropractors, naturopaths, personal trainers, coaches, physical therapists, and health insurance companies all play important roles, affecting the amount and quality of services. Patients project power through the services they choose to pay for, by communicating with their healthcare providers, and by proactively managing their health through diet and exercise. This sphere overlaps with a component of education.

FAMILY – PROJECTS POWER

- All of society proceeds from the family

There are entities that exist to serve the family sphere such as the Church, social services, family ministries, adoption agencies, etc. Your position within one of those entities determines the power that can be projected. For example, this power could consist of some combination of the following:

- Education
- Financial aid or resource aid
- Health-care and/or counseling
- Protection and legal services

The family unit also projects power. Within the family unit, projecting power depends upon your role. Are you a husband, a father, a wife, a mother, a son or a daughter, a niece or a nephew? Power can be projected through:

- Affection and words of affirmation
- Financial provision
- Physical care and support
- Chores
- Each family member's role in the other 6 spheres of society

THREE KEYS

For the kingdom minded Christian there are three key questions that help determine how to project power in order to enforce the will of King Jesus.

First, "What is your motivation?" If love[xxiv] is not your motivation, then whatever you do is little more than a dead work.

The second question is, "What would the kingdom look like in the area where you have responsibility and authority?" The answer to this empowers YOU to begin to identify a target, goal or destiny God has in store for your life.

The third question is, "Now that I have a goal in mind, how do I reach it? What is my strategy?" This is where the principles found in this book can equip and empower you to think, plan and pray like a strategic leader.

MEET THE AUTHOR OF STRATEGY

The Lord of Hosts is the author of strategy. He designed the principles of strategy, just as He designed the laws of gravity and aerodynamics. These principles can be learned. These principles work in any sphere.

I first applied these principles in the military. They worked! Then I tested them in the local church. They worked! Then I had the opportunity to apply them in the business world serving Fortune 100 companies like Ford, GM, GE, and HP. They worked fabulously! I became my company's "change management expert." Then I discovered that the same principles that work in corporations also work for sole proprietorships. From 2005 through 2010 I had the opportunity to help leaders apply these principles in cities and regions around the world with a goal of effecting real transformation. In fact, economies and crime rates were affected.   It worked!   We saw measurable results.

I have great confidence that any leader can learn these principles and apply them.   *My hope is to equip you to be a more effective strategic leader.*   These principles will prompt you to ask questions.   The answers will help you develop the best strategy for your situation.

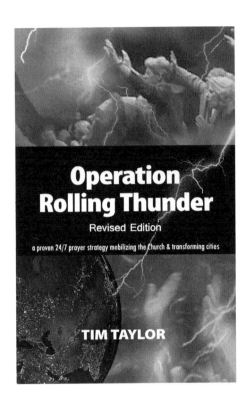

Operation Rolling Thunder
Revised Edition
a proven 24/7 prayer strategy mobilizing the church & transforming cities

TIM TAYLOR

ORT is a proven strategic mobilization plan that empowers local churches in a city or region to establish 24/7/365 prayer while establishing apostolic councils in all 7 spheres to transform their areas through the presentation of the gospel of the kingdom of our Lord Jesus Christ in power. Take the principles and theory you are learning in _Developing Apostolic Strategy_ and put them to practical use in your community today!

Order your copy at
www.KingdomLeague.org or _www.ORTPrayer.org_

WISDOM FOR BUILDING AND WAR

As a king, David oversaw all of the systems of the kingdom: a priestly system, a judicial system, an economic system, an agricultural system, and a governmental system which included a standing army of 24,000 warriors from each tribe. As the kingdom grew so did the systems. David's wisdom was demonstrated by his actions, as recorded in scripture. I believe King David taught King Solomon, his son, much of the wisdom he had gleaned. Solomon then recorded this wisdom in the book of Proverbs.

> *Wisdom is the principal thing, therefore get wisdom.*

We can learn much by studying the book of Proverbs, which teaches the importance of wisdom. It says that wisdom is the principal thing,[xxv] and that wisdom, understanding and knowledge belong to God.[xxvi] It also teaches us that a man of understanding seeks wise counsel[xxvii] and that wisdom for building and strategy for war are found in a multitude of counsel.[xxviii] Just as in former times, today's systems require effective structure and strategic plans, built on wisdom, understanding and knowledge.

The life of David illustrates Proverbs 24:3-6: there is wisdom in a multitude of counsel. In 1 Chronicles 11, all the leaders gathered together at Hebron to make David king. The next major step David took as king was to gather all the leaders together to consult with them to see if they wanted to bring the presence of God into their region. (1 Chronicles 13) The next three chapters in 1 Chronicles, 13-16, are devoted to describing how David, Israel and the Levites worked together to bring God's presence to the City of David on Mount Zion. I believe King David operated this way because, even before Isaiah prophesied that God is the source of wisdom, David knew how to access the source of all wisdom, understanding and knowledge.

> *Isaiah 9:6 for unto us a Child is born, Unto us a Son is given; And the government will be upon His shoulder. And His name will be called Wonderful, Counselor, Mighty God, Everlasting Father, Prince of Peace...*

> *Isaiah 11:2 The Spirit of the Lord shall rest upon Him, The Spirit of wisdom and understanding, The Spirit of counsel and might, The Spirit of knowledge and of the fear of the Lord.*

David wanted God's presence, in the presence of his councils. That is why he arranged for 24/7 prayer, praise and worship all year long on MT Zion in the City of David. He understood that God dwells in, is enthroned by, and is seated as a judge through continual prayer, praise and worship.

> *Psalm 22:3 But You are holy, Enthroned in the praises of Israel.*

> *Psalm 110:1-2 The Lord said to my Lord, "Sit at My right hand, till I make Your enemies Your footstool." The Lord shall send the rod of Your strength out of Zion. Rule in the midst of Your enemies!*

Understanding the importance of prayer and its role in bringing God's abiding presence to a community is at the heart of Operation Rolling Thunder (ORT); a strategy we've provided too many churches. Some mistake this for simply another prayer strategy. In reality ORT equips leaders to take the same first two steps King David took when he began to build his kingdom. It gathers leaders representing all seven spheres of society into councils where they are introduced to the basic strategic principles of war. All the while a resting place for God's presence is created in your city through 24/7 prayer, praise and worship. It is the continual prayer which invites the counsel of our Father, the author of strategy, into the leaders' councils.

Leaders representing all seven spheres form the councils. They seek God for His counsel asking, "What would the kingdom look like in this situation, geography or sphere?" An understanding of the principles presented in this book equips them to ask the right questions. The answers to those questions, with guidance from our Lord, give them wisdom to develop the most effective prayer and action strategies in each situation.

As an example of this, I'll share a story, but leave out some details for safety's sake. In May 2008 a leader in Pakistan utilized ORT to mobilize a certain city. It began with 24/7 prayer. Each church took one day because by cooperating they could cover the days quickly. The leaders found great insight and wisdom in God's presence. God gave them direction, which led to the making of Church history in Pakistan. In December 2008 I received letters from the government and from a jail superintendent, thanking us for helping to plant the first church ever in a prison in Pakistani history. How marvelous! All glory goes to our Lord Jesus Christ! However, this would not have occurred had the leaders not gleaned wisdom and then acted in faith. God gave the plan; His leaders implemented it; the people followed it, and historical results followed.

The Bible says there is wisdom and safety in a multitude of counsel.[xxix] The corporate world calls such efforts "think tanks" or "brain storming." There is no way that any one person can know everything. We are a lot smarter when we reason together rather than in isolation. 1 Corinthians 13:9 says that we know in part and prophesy in part. It is only when the parts are put together that you get the whole picture.

The whole picture often involves both war and building. King David had a war to fight and a kingdom to build. There are timeless principles of wisdom that apply to both. Both of these activities require wisdom, knowledge and understanding. I've discovered by studying these principles that throughout scripture wisdom, building and strategy for war are closely related. The relationship is consistent throughout both testaments.

Let's look at some examples of how these principles have worked in today's world. As a Naval Officer I studied the principles of war. The major principles of war have been taught to military leaders for over 2,500 years. They are taught because they work. As I personally studied them I discovered that they work because they are Biblically based.

During Desert Storm I had an opportunity to apply some of these principles to develop new operational procedures. Then, in 1992 through 1994 I had the opportunity to test these principles. I started with a church plant and mobilizing my first city. Measurable results were recorded pointing to transformation.

From 1999 to 2002 I had a chance to test the principles in a software company serving Fortune 100 companies. At one point I consulted for five of the Fortune 10 companies and equipped their leaders to develop rollout strategies, improve processes, design new curriculum, build new departments, and solve organizational and teamwork challenges. Later I used these principles while consulting with a sole proprietor who had just filed Chapter 13 bankruptcy. Within one year he saw a 127% increase in gross revenue. I've consulted with ministerial organizations that needed to revise their vision, mission, values and operational plans. I've used the principles to help new ministries and non-profits in the start-up phase. Since 2005 I've tested these principles around the world with resulting city transformation.

This is what I discovered:

- Biblical principles always work when applied.
- Understanding Biblical principles helps you ask the right questions.

- The answers to the questions help identify your strategy and where you need to seek counsel.
- The principles, applied with understanding, maximize the utilization of specialized knowledge.
- These principles are cross cultural and work in any sphere of society.

I have great confidence in these proven principles. I know any leader can learn them. I challenge you to learn them. Look for opportunities to apply them. Always start with the principle of objective and then go through each of the principles one by one. Effective strategies are not built on the application of one principle alone; the principles are always used in combination. Remember, it is wise to glean counsel and seek insight from others who are gifted strategists. Seek understanding and gather information. Compile the big picture.

Some in Christendom say, "We don't want man's plans, we just want to be led by God's Spirit." This is usually because they have seen the results of developing plans and programs without wisdom, understanding and God's guidance. If this experience is frequently repeated a leader can come to believe that any long term strategy or program is "man's plan." Sometimes these plans have been just that! However, the problem is not "planning," but planning without God's presence.

Look at some Biblical examples. Moses developed the plans for the tabernacle in the book of Exodus. Yet you certainly can't call those detailed plans "man's plans" even though they came through a man. God even gifted certain craftsmen to work from these plans with a spirit of wisdom so they could bring the vision God gave to Moses to fruition. King David spent years planning the temple which his son Solomon built. David had wisdom, understanding and knowledge. But, in 1 Chronicles 28:12 it says that David received the "plans for all he had by the Spirit." Don't mistake forethought, preparation or planning for "man's plans." In truth, these are an integral part of applying wisdom when combined with God's personal and daily guidance.

I am going to encourage you to do as I have done. Learn the principles and develop a daily personal relationship with the author, our heavenly Father. Invite His input into your counsel. Many times I have prayed in my office, asking the Lord for wisdom and insight into how to improve a process, solve a problem or create a new department based upon the principles I had studied. The principles helped me ask the right questions. Then, through wisdom and His guidance, He helped me develop solutions. Since Jesus taught us to pray "thy kingdom come and will be done on earth as it is in heaven," sometimes I'd say, "Lord I know there is no inefficiency in heaven, so how do I replicate that on earth?" Or, "What would this situation look like in heaven?" "What would heaven on earth look like in this company or for this client?" Then I would apply the principles one by one, continuing to ask for wisdom. I know that God has imparted to me a gift of wisdom. I pray that through the study of these principles you will exercise your faith for an impartation of that gift.

PRINCIPLE OF OBJECTIVE

Throughout the next chapters as we study the principles of war we will follow a certain pattern. First I will present what I studied while in the Navy; then I will provide the Biblical basis for each principle. Finally, we will look at some practical examples of how the principles have been applied.

Of all the principles I believe this first principle of objective is the most important. I am convinced that this one principle can dramatically change your life. It is one of the keys to turning a vision into reality and to solving difficult problems. *This principle is the critical starting place for developing an effective strategy.*

> *Objective is the first principle to be applied.*

The Navy taught me that:

1. The objective must be clearly defined.
2. The adversary must be destroyed.
3. The territory must be occupied.

BIBLICAL BASIS

What does the Bible say?

1. *Habakkuk 2:2 Write the vision down make it plain on the tablets so the herald can run with it.*
2. *1 John 3:8 For this purpose was the son of God manifested, that He might destroy the works of the devil.*

3. In Genesis 22:17 part of the Abrahamic promise is that his descendants would possess the gates of their enemies.
4. Jesus also told us in Luke 19:13 to "occupy till I come."

PRACTICAL APPLICATION

The objective must be clearly defined

Now it is time to break this principle down further and begin to learn the wisdom it has to offer. Recognize that this is an ongoing process. First the objective must be clearly defined. You must identify your target, or your goal. Here are some questions to help you begin to apply this principle:

- What is your vision?
- What is the mission?
- What is the scope of the problem?
- What is the goal?
- Is the objective written down so that others can communicate it clearly?

ADVERSARY DESTROYED OR OVERCOME

The second part of the principle of objective requires the destruction of, or the overcoming of, an adversary. Think of this as removing an obstacle that opposes you in reaching your goal. It could be people, a process, a system or a thing. Your enemy or adversary is that obstacle.

To develop the most effective strategy requires gathering intelligence about two very important things: your enemy and your allies. First, ask what opposes you in reaching the objective. What are the strengths, dispositions and strategies of the opposition? Second, ask who your allies are. What are their strengths, dispositions and capabilities?

Once these two questions are completely answered, a strategic leader will be equipped with the most up to date information. This information sets up the opportunity to develop the best possible strategy at that time. But the strategic plan is not complete until you have answered one more question. "How will we occupy this area long term after the adversary is overcome?"

OCCUPY

While destroying the enemy or overcoming the obstacle requires a warfare strategy, occupying a position long term requires a building plan, or a long term strategic plan. The process of occupying often moves us from an event into a long term process. Here are some questions that can help you explore this area.

1. How long do we need to occupy this place?
2. What skills and what kinds of people will this require?
3. What resources are needed?
4. What will it take to make this victory self-sustaining?

A TOOL TO EQUIP YOU APPLY THE PRINCIPLE

Ezekiel 22:30 says God seeks for a man to stand in the gap and build up a wall. I cannot tell you how often this scripture, combined with the following diagram, has helped me apply the principle of objective. It is a simple way to help you remember the basic order of the steps you need to apply to achieve the principle of objective.

First, you need to identify clearly your objective or goal. Second, you identify the baseline by determining what opposes you and who your allies are. Then you ask the question, "How will I get from the baseline to my objective? What steps will it take?"

Gap Analysis

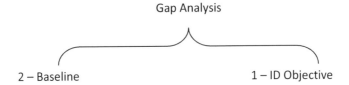

2 – Baseline   1 – ID Objective

Often I'll get with my council, or the leadership team with which I am consulting, and we'll diagram this on a white board and begin to brainstorm. In many cases we will discover that we cannot answer all of the questions right away. The answers may require research. At least, the process will have helped us identify what information is needed. Then the team can assign action items to appropriate people. They can then gather the required information, the analysis can be completed, and the principle can be applied in its entirety.

A consultant, or a strategic planner, can often be of great benefit. A good strategist understands the principles, how to facilitate teamwork and how to draw out of a team the answers and wisdom that reside inside them. If you or your team needs help developing or improving:

- Vision, mission and values
- Initial action plans
- A system or a process
- Teamwork
- Strategic leadership skills
- A new strategy

Visit www.KingdomLeague.org

Or contact Tim Taylor 425-687-0994

PRINCIPLE OF OFFENSE

Offense is the only way you achieve victory. Defense is important but it must be integrated with an offensive strategy. Defense alone simply avoids or delays defeat.

BIBLICAL BASIS

What does the Bible say?

- The kingdom of God suffers violence and the violent take it by force.[xxx]
- Show me your faith without your works and I'll show you my faith by my works; faith without works is dead.[xxxi]

King David understood the principle of offense well. We see in 2nd Samuel 5:7 that he took the stronghold of Zion first. He took Zion first because it was a stronghold and would be more easily defended. It was from this fortified place that he began to build the kingdom. He needed a strong base of operations from which to launch offensive operations. This was wise.

Offense is the only way to gain victory.

The principle of offense teaches us to be proactive. Vision and theory with no action is nothing more than an idea. Vision and theory accompanied by wise action result in creation: witty inventions, solutions, measurable results, and destiny.

The one who is on defense is at the mercy of the one who is on offense. The one on defense can only respond to offensive actions. The one on offense chooses the time, place and tactics used in any engagement.

I like what General George S. Patton said. "A good plan, violently executed now, is better than a perfect plan next week."[xxxii]

This reminds me of a meeting I had. A national ministry invited me and another very well-known speaker in the area of city transformation to advise them on a national strategy. They listened to the other man's input first. They loved his teaching, and so did I. As he was finishing his recommendation, I suddenly understood why my input was going to be radically different from his. He was a teacher and an analyst. His focus was on research and learning from what others had accomplished.

I began my recommendation by appreciating his teaching. Then I advised them that my input would be very different from his because he was an analyst and I was a catalyst. I would focus on the principles to apply to help them develop and launch an effective strategy.

Analysts are necessary. They are invaluable in gathering the detailed intelligence needed to apply the principle of objective. But analysts can get stuck in the "paralysis of analysis." You need to make sure you have a catalyst in the lead rather than an analyst.

PRACTICAL APPLICATION

In any endeavor it is wise to follow the example we find in 1 Corinthians 12:28 where it says that God set apostles first, prophets second and teachers third. This is an order of function. The apostolic and prophetic gifts are both examples of catalysts for city transformation. The apostolic gift and the prophetic gift both carry a revelatory anointing. Revelation is essential to knowing *what* to do. In addition to revelation, the apostle carries a gift of wisdom to know *how* to do something. Apostles are gifted by God with strategy, wisdom and understanding. Ideally, these are the catalysts that should lead and initiate offensive actions. This is because they carry the blue prints, so to speak, from which all the other sub-contractors (prophet, teacher, pastor, and evangelist) work.

PRINCIPLE OF MASS

Mass is one of the most important principles because it defines combat power. Mass is determined by a number of factors, which include:

1. Leadership
2. Morale and resolution of the troops
3. Fighting ability and tactical skills
4. Discipline
5. Number of weapons

Mass defines power.

Mass is a concentration of power to be applied at a decisive point; that is the point of maximum effectiveness. The decisive point is the target. By applying the principle of objective you gather the information needed to determine your allies' capabilities and determine the amount of power you have to project. Next, intelligence is gathered regarding the adversary, which helps identify the target, or the decisive point, where the power is to be applied. The goal is to use just enough power to accomplish the mission or reach the objective. This concept is called "economy of force."

BIBLICAL BASIS

What does the Bible say?

1. Leadership – The fivefold ministry was given to equip the saints and the apostolic gift was given for strategy.[xxxiii]

2. Morale – God has not given us a spirit of fear but of love, power and a sound mind.[xxxiv]
3. Fighting ability and tactical skills – Be strong in the Lord and in the power of His might, put on the whole armor of God that you may be able to withstand the wiles of the devil.[xxxv]
4. Discipline – The root word of discipline is disciple. Jesus commanded us to "go and make disciples."[xxxvi]
5. Number of weapons - The Bible models the principle of mass where it says that five will chase a hundred and a hundred will put ten thousand to flight; one puts a thousand to flight and two put ten thousand to flight.[xxxvii]

Economy of force is demonstrated a number of times in the Bible. The goal of economy of force is to use the minimum force necessary to accomplish the mission. Gideon is probably the most well-known Biblical example of this concept. The army of Israel was fighting against an enemy force of about 135,000. 120,000 of the enemy fell in the first engagement, leaving 15,000. God reduced Gideon's force from about 30,000 down to 300. Those 300 chased the remaining 15,000.[xxxviii] Now that, my friends, is economy of force!

PRACTICAL APPLICATION

Remember, the role of an army is to project power in order to enforce the will of its government. The Church is the army of the Lord and we are called to project power into all spheres of society. Identifying your objective, your allies and what opposes your goal in each sphere will help you determine the power you can project to effect change. One key to success here is a transformed mind.[xxxix] I encourage you to pray and to ask God for wisdom as to how you can apply each of these principles in your life.

Principle of Communication and Supply

Communication lines and supply lines are one and the same. In the military, they involve all routes of sea, air, and land which join a fighting force with its base of operations. Along these routes, orders, supplies, and reinforcements flow. Ample supplies must continually move along these routes until an enemy is defeated and the war is won.

Biblical Basis

This concept is illustrated in the Bible via the Greek word "koinania." This is often translated fellowship between God and man. But it also means partnership, to communicate and to distribute.[xi] I'll bold the Greek word koinania as translated in each scripture below.

- 1 John 1:3 That which we have seen and heard declare we unto you, that ye also may have **fellowship** with us: and truly our **fellowship** is with the Father, and with his Son Jesus Christ. KVJ
- Hebrew 13:16 But to do good and to **communicate** forget not: for with such sacrifices God is well pleased. KVJ
- 2 Corinthians 9:13   While by the experiment of this ministration they glorify God for your professed subjection unto the gospel of Christ, and for your liberal **distribution** unto them, and unto all men; KVJ
- Romans 15:26 For it hath pleased them of Macedonia and Achaia to make a certain **contribution** for the poor saints which are at Jerusalem. KJV

Truly communication lines and supply lines are one and the same. This is so in every sphere of society – especially in the Church.

There are several important elements of the principle of communication. First, communication must be clear. This is essential for teamwork and for coordinating any sort of large scale or joint actions. Second, clarity involves not only the lines of communications but also the actual means of communication, such as language and method of transmission. In the military we refer to this as communication protocol.

> *Communication & supply lines are one and the same.*

The Army, Navy, Air Force and Marines each have a unique culture and their own methods of communicating. Up until the early 80s there were challenges with joint-operations because each service had their own communication protocols. This issue was highlighted during an operation in Haiti in the early 80s. An army unit was pinned down on a beach. They could easily see a naval vessel right off shore but they could not communicate with them because the communication systems did not work with each other. A shrewd army officer solved the problem by using a payphone to call a friend in the Pentagon. The friend relayed the situation and coordinates to the Navy. The Navy eventually communicated with the ship enabling them to provide fire support.

These types of communication challenges were ultimately solved. A common communication protocol was instituted, allowing different military organizations to connect, communicate and coordinate their efforts. They recognized that their communication lines and supply lines were one and the same.

PRACTICAL APPLICATION

The Church faces a similar challenge today. We need to communicate among various ministries, churches and organizations representing different denominations, skills and abilities. Each has varying degrees of focus in cites, regions, states and nations. The Lord originally spoke to me regarding this challenge in 1991 during Desert Storm and again in 1993. He communicated to me that there would come a day when the Body of Christ would need to connect in the same way the US Army, Navy, Air Force and Marines connected with our 38 allies during Desert Storm.

I served on the staff of the admiral that oversaw the war for the Navy. Besides advising him on my area of expertise, I also stood watch in his operations center. Through this experience God gave me the strategy for CONECT (Christian Outreach Network Establishing City-wide Teamwork). CONECT is a common communication protocol designed to facilitate teamwork and joint operations in the Body of Christ as we work together to transform cities, states and nations. CONECT is based on the patterns that King David, Nehemiah and King Hezekiah modeled. In CONECT leaders are provided a strategy which enables their teams to develop a strong base of operations from which to launch their offensive operations. It enables them to establish a strategic communication center, an operations center, and a command post, or a war room.

When communication is cut, an army loses direction and morale decreases.

Communication is essential to applying the other principles, such as:

- Objective
    o Assisting in gathering intelligence
- Mass and offense
    o Coordinating efforts with allies to increase power

The final element we need to address is the concept of "command and control." Communication is key to coordinating large groups for strategic action. If an army is cut off from its commanding officer it is probable that within a short time the coordinated action and force of the army will deteriorate. The army will lose direction and morale will begin to fail. If you understand this principle you will understand why communication centers are usually attacked first in any military engagement. This teaches us first that we need to protect our communication lines, and second that we should seek to disrupt our adversaries' communication.

Finally, command and control teaches that spheres of authority and responsibility should be defined clearly so that it is apparent who makes decisions. Communication and orders should flow through a single point of contact in each unit or organization.

Principle of Mobility

Mobility, or movement, speaks of the way combat forces move to engage an enemy. When an army cannot move, it cannot attack, retreat or evade. It can only defend itself.

As you recall, principles and strategies never change. Only the weapons change. I will add one more idiom: the manner in which the principles are combined together to form a strategy constantly change. Once a strategy is developed and a campaign is launched, the situation is dynamic. We do our very best to plan, strategize, and develop contingency plans based on what our adversary might do. But it is difficult to anticipate everything. This aspect of the unknown is called "the fog of war." It means that once a battle has begun we need to be prepared to adapt. We must be ready to adjust our tactical plans and overall strategy based on up to date intelligence.

This highlights the role and importance of a robust secure communication system that supports intelligence gathering, command and control. This empowers leaders to effectively combine the other principles. For example, mobility is directly related to offense because offense requires the ability to move and initiate action. Defense is important but it should be planned with offensive action in mind.

Biblical Basis

What does the Bible say? How does it illustrate the principle of mobility?

- In Judges 14:4 God sought to initiate an offensive action. He "was seeking an occasion to move against the Philistines."
- Numbers 2 describes the order and manner in which the tribes and the Ark of the Covenant should "move out."[xli]

- In the great commission, Jesus commands his disciples to "go and make disciples."[xlii]

Obeying the command that Jesus gave us in the great commission requires utilizing the principle of offense and mobility. First an action has to be initiated. This may require moving from person to person, from house to house, from city to city, or from nation to nation.

PRACTICAL APPLICATION

Mobility is also related to the delivery of power, or mass. How mobility and power are applied depends upon the sphere in which we are operating. Mobility might require the distribution or sending of communication, prayer, money, resources, or people. Mobility is closely related to the principle of communication and supply, as well as to offense.

Rarely is one principle applied alone. A strategy involves these core principles being applied in combination and integrated with each other in varying and dynamic degrees, because war or conflict is dynamic. Once a great plan is launched, it often needs to be changed – a little or a lot, depending upon the adversary's response. The objective rarely changes unless it is obtained. But the combination of principles applied in a given strategy often changes to adapt to new circumstances. Hence, every leader who desires to be effective ought to learn these principles and learn them well. There are three ways to learn them.

- Study books like this.
- Acquire personal mentors.
- Develop a personal daily relationship with the author of strategy, our Heavenly Father, the Lord of Hosts.

Principle of Surprise

The principle of surprise is obtained in any engagement with an adversary when you attack suddenly without warning. The effect of surprise leaves the enemy feeling astonished or dumbfounded. This principle is applied in conjunction with other principles. For example, the principle of objective teaches us that we need to gather intelligence on our adversary while keeping our location, intention and capability concealed. The principle of surprise also interacts with mass and plays a key role in applying economy of force. Surprise often allows the offense to accomplish their objective with fewer men and materials when the appropriate amount of force is applied at a decisive point.

Surprise is obtained when an adversary is attacked suddenly without warning.

There are three elements required to plan the use of surprise. These elements are:

1. Time
2. Place
3. Tactic

Biblical Basis

How is this principle illustrated in the Bible? Gideon is a perfect example of a timid leader who trusted a great strategic planner. He trusted the author of strategy, the Lord of Hosts; and His principles of war. Following our Lord's direction he first applied the principle of objective and spied out the enemy camp. Based on his intelligence findings and at the direction of the Lord, he began reducing his army from over 30,000 to 300. He chose the time (middle watch). Then he chose the tactic, which was to divide 300 men with pitchers, torches, rams' horns, and a word into 3 companies. On his command they were to break the pitchers, sound the rams' horns and yell, "The sword of the Lord and of Gideon." The place was determined by assigning troops to certain locations surrounding the enemy camp.[xliii] Such amazing surprise was achieved that 120,000 of 135,000 perished in the first engagement. Then only 300 continued on to chase the remaining 15,000.

PRACTICAL APPLICATION

This is a good time to revisit the principle of mass. Gideon utilized this principle and exercised excellent leadership and strategic planning. The morale and discipline of the troops was reflected during the selection process at the river, and was further demonstrated as these troops faithfully executed the plan and chased the enemy. The number of weapons was 300 men, 300 torches, 300 pitchers, and 300 rams' horns. Gideon's execution of the plan God gave him allowed this small number to project enough power to accomplish the objective.

In addition, there are a number of other principles in play here. They include objective, offense, mass, mobility, communication/supply, security, simplicity and surprise. This battle is a beautiful example of economy of force which would not have been possible without utilizing the principle of surprise.

Principle of Simplicity

The principle of simplicity indicates that military planning should be kept as simple as possible. Unity of command is another important aspect of simplicity, requiring a clear chain of command and clear communication. In addition, orders should never be ambiguous and frequent changes of plans should be avoided.

> *Keep planning as simple as possible.*

Biblical Basis

Chapter one of Joshua provides a great example of the unity of command through a clear chain of command. God spoke to Joshua, Joshua commanded the officers, and the officers passed through the camp and commanded the people. *The order was simple – clear and concise – and it provided the time frame in which they were to be prepared to execute certain parts of the order.*

> *Joshua 1:11 Pass through the camp and command the people, saying, 'Prepare provisions for yourselves, for within three days you will cross over this Jordan, to go in to possess the land which the Lord your God is giving you to possess.*

The chain of command was clear, as well. The people responded to the officers as if they represented Joshua.

> *Joshua 1:16 All that you command us we will do, and wherever you send us we will go. NKJV*

How was this chain of command originally determined? Exodus 18 gives us a glimpse of the chain of command that God instructed Moses to put into place to organize the nation of Israel. A chain of command was required to execute the people's coordinated movements through the wilderness, to communicate effectively and to distribute the task of making decisions (judging).

The following scriptures demonstrate the need for concise decisions and clear communication.

James 1:7-8 For let not that man suppose that he will receive anything from the Lord; he is a double-minded man, unstable in all his ways.

1 Kings 18:21 And Elijah came to all the people, and said, "How long will you falter between two opinions? If the Lord is God, follow Him; but if Baal, follow him." But the people answered him not a word.

Matthew 5:37 But let your 'Yes' be 'Yes,' and your 'No,' 'No.' For whatever is more than these is from the evil one.

PRACTICAL APPLICATION

Unity of command is an important aspect of the principle of simplicity. It says that there should be a clear chain of command where authority is determined by responsibility. One in a position of responsibility should be delegated enough authority to fulfill their assignment. One in command must also have a servant's heart, character, courage and the ability to lead.

COMMUNICATION, COMMAND AND CONFUSION

Communication is intertwined closely with unity of command and the principle of simplicity. It is important for each person on a team to report to only one person and to avoid taking orders or direction from anyone who is not so delegated. Team members should not take direction from someone who has no responsibility, for that person has no authority. If unity of command is violated through poor communication, inevitably confusion is introduced. While a poor communication process introduces confusion, *lack of communication* produces *vain imaginations*. Designating a single point of communication reduces confusion and maximizes efficiency.

The way to manage communication is through a common protocol. Unity of command is the key to establishing clear communications. The larger the organization, the more complex it becomes and the more important these principles become. Understanding this is critical to mobilizing and coordinating large masses of people effectively to project power. So, IF, (and note that is a big IF), these principles are applied well, then growing, mobilizing and coordinating large organizations is not only possible, but relatively simple.

> *Clear communication lines with a single point of contact are essential to avoid confusion and apply simplicity*

Remember that God is called Lord of the Armies (Hosts) more than 245 times in the Bible. He is the one who organizes His army for war. Jesus taught us to pray, "thy kingdom come and will be done on earth as it is in heaven." In heaven, there is order, and clear communication. These principles are part of the kingdom.[xliv]

One example of this heavenly organization on earth begins when all authority was given to Jesus.[xlv] Jesus received all authority because of His responsibility to redeem mankind. Upon his accession into heaven He sent the Holy Spirit. Through the Holy Spirit further gifts and responsibilities were distributed to people, as described in Ephesians 4:7-16, Romans 12:1-9, and 1 Corinthians 12:1-12.

There are several illustrations of the unity of command in the Bible. For example, God did not ask us to vote on the great commission. In addition, God Himself has determined the time and territory each person is called to effect.[xlvi] Throughout Paul's epistles to Timothy and Titus we find the delegation of responsibility and authority. Eleven times the apostle Paul directs young ministers of the gospel of Jesus Christ to command, charge or rebuke. His job and theirs was to bring order to the emergent church. The principle of unity of command and the principle of simplicity are alive and clear in the New Testament.

Lord, I pray that you give us a revelation of your name as the Lord of Hosts. I believe a revelation of that name will revolutionize how we function as the Body of Christ and operate together in the days to come.

PRINCIPLE OF SECURITY

The principle of security includes all measures taken to guard an army against surprise attacks and to ensure the protection of the people. Guarding against surprise attacks requires two things:

1. To know the strengths, plans and location of the enemy forces arrayed against your army.
2. To keep information concerning your army's strengths, plans and location secret from your adversary.

BIBLICAL BASIS

The Bible warns us to "be on your guard; stand firm in the faith; be men of courage; be strong"[xlvii] and to "be sober, be vigilant; because your adversary the devil walks about like a roaring lion, seeking whom he may devour. Resist him, steadfast in the faith."[xlviii] We find other aspects of the principle of security illustrated through the following scriptures:

> *Security includes all measures taken to guard an army or people against surprise attacks.*

- *Hosea 4:6 My people are destroyed for lack of knowledge.*
- *2 Corinthians 2:11 ...lest Satan should take advantage of us; for we are not ignorant of his devices.*

I have witnessed a real challenge in regards to security in the Body of Christ in the area of discretion; especially the ability to keep from talking too much. There is an idiom in the Navy that says "loose lips sink ships." This phrase originated in WWII when sailors on leave from their ships might talk about where they had been or where they were headed. To have loose lips means you talk too much. Inadvertently revealing sensitive information could enable the enemy to sabotage a ship's or convoy's mission. This could endanger not only the mission but also the lives of your shipmates and possibly even others. The Bible says:

- *Proverbs 10:19 In the multitude of words sin is not lacking, but he who restrains his lips is wise.*
- *Psalm 141:3 Set a guard, O Lord, over my mouth; keep watch over the door of my lips.*

There is also an example in Isaiah 39 which illustrates this principle well. The king of Babylon heard that King Hezekiah had been sick and had recovered. So he sent his emissaries to deliver a letter to him. Then Hezekiah did a very foolish thing. He showed these emissaries EVERYTHING. He showed them the silver, gold, treasuries, spices, precious ointment and even his armory. The emissaries not only knew what treasure was there and where it was, but they also saw the king's weapons and how his forces were deployed. Look at what God says in Isaiah 39:7.

> *Then Isaiah the prophet went to King Hezekiah, and said to him, "What did these men say, and from where did they come to you?" So Hezekiah said, "They came to me from a far country, from Babylon." And he said, "What have they seen in your house." So Hezekiah answered, "They have seen all that is in my house; there is nothing among my treasures that I have not shown them." Then Isaiah said to Hezekiah, "Hear the word of the Lord of hosts: 'Behold, the days are coming when all that is in your house, and what your fathers have accumulated until this day, shall be carried to Babylon; nothing shall be left,' says the Lord. 'And they shall take away some of your sons who will descend from you, whom you will beget; and they shall be eunuchs in the palace of the king of Babylon.'"*

PRACTICAL APPLICATION

The exercise of discretion is vital. In response to this need, the military has security clearances. There are different levels of security that range from confidential, to secret, top secret and beyond. Each level of clearance has rules that describe how that information is to be handled. There are three critical elements of a security clearance that we need to look at.

1. Performing a background check
2. Monitoring an individual's actions to ensure compliance
3. Applying consequences for noncompliance

In 1 Samuel 16, King Saul had his servants bring David to play music because of a distressing spirit. David served in the presence of the king. The king knew who David was. Yet, after David killed Golaith, the king ordered a background check.

> I Samuel 17:55-16 When Saul saw David going out against the Philistine, he said to Abner, the commander of the army, "Abner, whose son is this youth." And Abner said, "As your soul lives, O king, I do not know." So the king said, "Inquire whose son this young man is."

Saul did this because he wanted to bring David into a closer working relationship with him and the kingdom.

What else does the Bible teach?

- *1 Thessalonians 5:21 Prove all things; hold fast that which is good. KJV*
- *2 Timothy 2:2 And the things that you have heard from me among many witnesses, commit these to faithful men.*
- *John 2:24 But Jesus did not commit Himself to them, because He knew all men.*

- *1 Thessalonians 5:12 But we beseech you, brethren, to know them that labor among you, and are over you in the Lord, and admonish you; ASV*

Security is critical whether your sphere of responsibility involves the family, church, government, business, media, health-care, or education. I pray God gives you wisdom to apply the principle of security.

JESUS AND THE PRINCIPLES

Jesus is the captain of our salvation and the Commander of the hosts of heaven.[xlix] If anyone needs to be equipped with wisdom for strategy it would be the Commander of the hosts of heaven. I have found plenty of evidence that God the Father, the author of strategy, taught Jesus, His Son, these principles. Listed below you will find each principle followed by where you see the principle applied.

THE PRINCIPLE OF OBJECTIVE

The objective must be clearly defined. In Matthew 24:30-31 the Lord directs the angels to gather the elect.

> *Matthew 24:30-31 Then the sign of the Son of Man will appear in heaven, and then all the tribes of the earth will mourn, and they will see the Son of Man coming on the clouds of heaven with power and great glory. And He will send His angels with a great sound of a trumpet, and they will gather together His elect from the four winds, from one end of heaven to the other.*

The second part of objective teaches us that the enemy must be destroyed. 1 John 3:8 illustrates this. "For this purpose the Son of God was manifested, that He might destroy the works of the devil."

The third part of the principle of objective deals with long term occupation. God is preparing a bride for His son and Jesus went to prepare a place for us that we might dwell with Him.

John 14:3 And if I go and prepare a place for you, I will come again and receive you to Myself; that where I am, there you may be also.

Revelation 21:2-4 Then I, John, saw the holy city, New Jerusalem, coming down out of heaven from God, prepared as a bride adorned for her husband. And I heard a loud voice from heaven saying, "Behold, the tabernacle of God is with men, and He will dwell with them, and they shall be His people. God Himself will be with them and be their God.

THE PRINCIPLE OF OFFENSE

Offense is the only way to gain victory. Defense only avoids or delays defeat. Jesus commanded His disciples to initiate action.

Matthew 28:18-19 And Jesus came and spoke to them, saying, "All authority has been given to Me in heaven and on earth. Go therefore and make disciples of all the nations, baptizing them in the name of the Father and of the Son and of the Holy Spirit."

THE PRINCIPLE OF MASS

Mass defines power. One of the factors of mass is numbers. Jesus will return with an army of angels and saints, as illustrated in the following scriptures.

2 Thessalonians 1:6-8 ...since it is a righteous thing with God to repay with tribulation those who trouble you, and to give you who are troubled rest with us when the Lord Jesus is revealed from heaven with His mighty angels, in flaming fire taking vengeance on those who do not know God, and on those who do not obey the gospel of our Lord Jesus Christ.

Jude 14   Now Enoch, the seventh from Adam, prophesied about these men also, saying, "Behold, the Lord comes with ten thousands of His saints."

THE PRINCIPLE OF COMMUNICATION AND SUPPLY AND MOBILITY

The action of our Lord's is initiated with a sign in heaven. Then the trumpet signals that it is time for the angels to gather the elect. Everyone will see the Lord on the move. This communication initiates offensive action.

Matthew 24:30-31   Then the sign of the Son of Man will appear in heaven, and then all the tribes of the earth will mourn, and they will see the Son of Man coming on the clouds of heaven with power and great glory. And He will send His angels with a great sound of a trumpet, and they will gather together His elect from the four winds, from one end of heaven to the other.

THE PRINCIPLE OF SECURITY AND SURPRISE

Surprise cannot be attained without security. Security is gained through knowing what your adversary is doing and by keeping your own intentions secret. That is why the Lord commands His people to watch and be alert.

Mark 13:32-33 But of that day and hour no one knows, not even the angels in heaven, nor the Son, but only the Father. Take heed, watch and pray; for you do not know when the time is.

Revelation 3:3 Remember therefore what you have received and heard; hold fast and repent. Therefore if you will not watch, I will come upon you as a thief, and you will not know what hour I will come upon you.

1 Corinthians 2:7-8 But we speak the wisdom of God in a mystery, the hidden wisdom which God ordained before the ages for our glory, which none of the rulers of this age knew; for had they known, they would not have crucified the Lord of glory.

THE PRINCIPLE OF SIMPLICITY

The bottom line in the principle of simplicity is to keep everything as uncomplicated and clear as possible. In Matthew 22 Jesus summarizes both the law and the prophets into two easy to remember commands.

Matthew 22:37-40 Jesus said to him, "You shall love the Lord your God with all your heart, with all your soul, and with all your mind. This is the first and great commandment. And the second is like it: You shall love your neighbor as yourself. On these two commandments hang all the Law and the Prophets."

Our heavenly Father is the author of these principles. It is clear that His son understands them. Now let's take a look at a couple of examples of how these principles have been used in ministry and business so you can begin to catch a vision for using these principles to fulfill   your   destiny.

WISDOM APPLIES THE PRINCIPLES

In Ephesians 1 Paul prayed that God would provide a spirit of wisdom and revelation. Revelation can disclose God's heart, purpose, special knowledge, directions or instructions about people, things and situations. However, revelation without application often leads to frustration. This is where the principles come in. They provide wisdom and help leaders move from theory to effective action combined with faith.

Wisdom is one of the keys to bringing prophetic words to fulfillment. We need to wage strategic warfare with the prophetic words that have gone before[l] us. Warfare begins with prayer that must be followed with faith in action.[li] Without faith in action, often a prophetic word remains waiting to be fulfilled.[lii]

For example, God gave me an operational plan called Operation Rolling Thunder in December 2004. The spirit of revelation revealed to other leaders and to me that I was to lead Washington State prayer. Using the principles, I devised an effective mobilization plan that aided leaders to the same principles city by city, county by county and state by state. As Operation Rolling Thunder spread across my state, we began to see the fulfillment of prophetic words spoken in 2003 by Dutch Sheets and Chuck Pierce, as well as numerous supernatural manifestations. These prophetic words remained latent until they were fulfilled by God's people acting in faith with wisdom. Let's take a look at how the principles of war are applied in Operation Rolling Thunder.

A MINISTRY EXAMPLE

Operation Rolling Thunder (ORT) is a mobilization strategy that supports establishing 24/7 prayer, praise and worship city by city in the spirit of the restoration of David's tabernacle.[liii] It also mobilizes the army of the Lord while gathering leaders representing all 7 spheres of society at the gates (places of authority) in a city.[liv] The continual prayer invites God's abiding presence and positions people to hear God's voice. It brings the Spirit of Counsel into councils of leaders representing each of the 7 spheres of society within a specific geography. This is the revelation – the revealing of God's heart and desire. The principles are applied to help glean wisdom and to develop effective action strategies. Here is an example of how ORT applies some of the principles you have learned.

OBJECTIVE

A review of the principle of objective first reminds us that we need a clearly defined goal. Next, we need to discover what opposes that goal, who our allies are, and what their capabilities are. Finally, we need to plan to occupy long term.

The overall objective is to "transform a city, county, state or nation through the presentation of the gospel of the kingdom of our Lord Jesus Christ." There are smaller objectives that support this overall goal. The first supporting objective is to form councils of kingdom minded leaders representing all 7 spheres of society. The second is to establish 24/7/365 prayer within a defined territory. These objectives follow the first two steps that King David took when he began to establish his kingdom.

Finally, ORT begins with the National Day of Prayer (NDP) and continues until the Global Day of Prayer (GDOP). Recognizing the strategic opportunity provided by mass, (numbers of people), the strategy encourages building NDP events and GDOP events while connecting both with 24/7 prayer. The prayer aspect is accomplished by asking local churches to take responsibility for one day of prayer in between these events.

In 2006 these prayer events were 31 days apart. Therefore we had our CONECTers identify 31 churches within their communities who would each take responsibility for one day during that time period. By cooperating, it was easy to mobilize 24/7 prayer. It was also easy to sustain the prayer should the churches choose to "occupy" the mountain of the Lord's house all year long.[iv]

The councils representing all 7 spheres initiate a process of discovery to gather spiritual intelligence about what opposes the gospel in each sphere and identify who their allies might be. When these steps are completed, leaders with appropriate jurisdiction are positioned to develop the very best prayer and action strategies for that strategic time.

MASS

Why is the timing of ORT a strategic time? It is because of the principle of mass. If you understand mass, you'll recognize the incredible power that is available to be harnessed and directed during NDP and GDOP. This is an opportune time for one church, or several churches in a city, to rout our adversary the devil and to make local gains for the kingdom, while supporting national and international prayer strategies orchestrated by the Holy Spirit. Every single person we can add dramatically increases the available power, since one person puts a thousand to flight and two ten thousand.[lvi] *I certainly hope everyone will recognize this opportunity and choose to cooperate putting their faith into action.*

OFFENSE

Offense is the only way to gain victory. ORT harnesses the momentum from NDP and GDOP. It moves congregations from isolated events to a long term campaign to occupy the Lord's house of prayer in their city or region by strategically coordinating prayer and action all year long. Most churches are too small to do this on their own, but by cooperating they can achieve 24/7 prayer quickly. This puts our adversary on the defense. He must react to us rather than the other way around.

COMMUNICATION AND SUPPLY

Communication lines and supply lines are one and the same. We recognize that the best way to increase power within a city or a region requires coordinated communication. ORT has a strategic communication plan that equips CONECTers (prayer leaders) to serve strategic leaders. It facilitates 24/7 prayer while sending watchmen and intercessors out to do research, prayer walks or to just hear and report what God is saying. These reports combined with the intelligence the councils provide to give the leaders representing all 7 spheres the overall picture about the situation. Then the leaders seek God for His strategy for their community within their spheres. These actions can initiate the forming of a strategic operations/ communications center, or war-room. Intelligence is gathered along the same lines used to mobilize and coordinate prayer and action, whether by churches or individuals. I could continue going through each principle, but suffice it to say, the system works.

In 2010, I assisted leaders in 31 nations to mobilize and connect the Church in their cities or regions through ORT. This strategy has been marked by documented signs, wonders and measurable results such as:

- Increased salvations and water baptisms
- Interaction with leaders from all 7 spheres including presidential and gubernatorial campaigns, state representatives, mayors, police chiefs, sheriffs, business leaders, principals, teachers, doctors, etc. to form Transformation Task Forces
- Decreased crime in numerous cities
- Increased revenue or decreased unemployment
- Droughts broken
- Decreased abortions while adoptions increased
- Reconciliation between people groups

To hear more great testimonies and learn how you can transform your city visit www.KingdomLeague.org or www.ORTPrayer.org.

Business Applies the Principles

In 1999 I was provided an opportunity to apply these principles in the software industry serving Fortune 100 companies like Ford, GM, GE, and HP. These principles helped me succeed. It is my hope that, as I share my testimony, you will begin to see how these principles can equip you to develop strategic solutions for your business or company. Understanding these strategic, Biblical, leadership principles helped me move quickly into a position of leadership in a young software company as a training manager. The principles helped me ask the right questions of my heavenly Father and of other people who had specialized knowledge. God gave me wisdom and favor. In a short time I turned around a failing training department and made it profitable.

Then VPs of various divisions began to ask me to help their directors, managers and teams to solve their organizational, operational and process issues. Whether the problems were large or small, the principles, combined with my personal relationship with my heavenly Father, helped me solve them all. One success would lead to a request for help on a greater challenge and that success would lead to additional opportunities.

The larger the problems I solved, the more I saw my financial compensation increase. I set financial goals when I began, which included raises and the timing of those raises. In four years I hit every single financial goal at the high end of the range I set.

During that time I received the revelation that I could be a minister and a business man all at the same time. It was liberating and refreshing to know that I could serve God as His minister in the business world or in any other sphere of society He might place me. Within a relatively short time I became my company's "change management expert." I had very little formal training in change management, but I did have a solid understanding of God's principles and a daily personal relationship with my heavenly Father, the author of those principles.

The GM Example

In time my company began to have me consult with project managers who were responsible for implementing the service we provided. I also consulted with our customers. Due to the growing volume of customers and rollouts, I developed training to teach leaders (project managers, directors, and VP's) a couple of principles so they were better equipped to help us rollout out our services. Here is one example of how these principles helped us create profitable solutions.

My company had two problems with GM. First, as customers they were dissatisfied because it had taken 13 months to rollout the first version of our service to them. The second problem was our Return on Investment (ROI). We did not get paid until the rollout was complete, so the longer it took the more it cost my company. The objective was to:

- Reduce the rollout time
- Satisfy our customer
- Increase our ROI

GM sent a VP, a director, and several project managers that my department was responsible to train. My staff assisted in teaching how to use our product/service, while I focused on teaching about the principles of objective and communication. The objective was clearly defined. Our customer wanted the rollout time reduced from 13 months. The second aspect of objective required that we identify what opposed the objective, who our allies were, and what their capabilities were. Our allies consisted of:

- A GM VP, a director and various project managers.

Our adversaries were:

- 40,000 employees who were accustomed to the old way of doing things and the natural human resistance to change.
- The 40,000 employees were located in 5 countries with different cultures.

Once the project managers understood the principles, we utilized an online survey to help us glean more intelligence. We discovered two main things. First the employees only heard about how our service benefited the corporation. They did not understand how it would benefit them personally. Secondly, culture was a major issue. For example the work culture in Japan is different from the culture in Australia. So the GM project managers designed a communication strategy that highlighted the personal benefits to each employee, while taking into consideration the specific country where they were rolling out the service. In Japan the communication could be fairly directive in nature, while in Australia the message was designed to win over the employees by highlighting how the change would greatly improve business life.

GM RESULTS

This strategy proved to be a win/win solution. GM was happy because:

- The rollout was reduced from 13 months to 4.5 months
- The GM VP wanted to enter retirement on a winning note and he was delighted to do just that
- The GM Director was promoted to VP
- My company was happy because we had a satisfied customer and we earned about $3 million. Many involved in the project received bonuses as well.

BIBLICAL PRINCIPLES WORK

I have used these principles to develop solutions for sole proprietorships, small businesses, non-profits, churches, ministries, organizations and the military. Biblical principles work when applied.

I have strong conviction that anyone can learn these principles and discover how to apply them. *It is my sincere hope that, through your study and application of these principles, you will be equipped to think, plan and pray strategically like an admiral, a general or an apostle. I pray that God will give you a spirit of wisdom and revelation so you can use these principles to fulfill your destiny in Christ.*

Sometimes a fresh set of eyes from outside counsel can be helpful. Perhaps you, your business or ministry is in need of a consultant to help:

- Develop strategic plans
- Develop vision, mission and values
- Develop or improve operational plans
- Develop or improve organizational plans
- Improve processes
- Develop a strategic communication plan
- Improve teamwork and organizational efficiency

If you would like Tim Taylor's help email commander@kingdomleague.org or call Tim's office at 425-687-0994.

ENDNOTES

The Function of the Apostolic Gift Today

[i] Jeremiah 1:5-10, 2 Corinthians 10:3-4, and Ephesians 2:20
[ii] Exodus 28:3, Exodus 31:3
[iii] Proverbs 24:3-6
[iv] Matthew 10:41
[v] Isaiah 56:7
[vi] Acts 15:16-17
[vii] Acts 6:3-4 and 2 Corinthians 12:1-6
[viii] Titus 1:5, Acts 14:23, and Ephesians 2:19-22
[ix] Acts 13 through Acts 15:30-41, Acts 21:10-11
[x] 2 Corinthians 12:12 and Hebrews 2:4
[xi] 2 Corinthians 10:3-4
[xii] 2 Corinthians 10:13, 13:2 and 1 Timothy 1:20

Projecting Power into Every Sphere

[xiii] Joel 2:1-10, Ezekiel 37:1-10, 2 Corinthians 3:10-4, and Ephesians 6:12
[xiv] 2 Samuel 1:3
[xv] Genesis 22:14
[xvi] Exodus 15:26
[xvii] 2 Corinthians 10:3-4, 1 Corinthians 3:10 and Jeremiah 1:5-10
[xviii] Biblesoft's New Exhaustive Strong's Numbers and Concordance with Expanded Greek-Hebrew Dictionary. Copyright © 1994, 2003, 2006 Biblesoft, Inc. and International Bible Translators, Inc. 4754 - strateuomai (strat-yoo'-om-ahee); middle voice from the base of NT:4756; to serve in a military campaign; figuratively, to execute the apostolate (with its arduous duties and functions), to contend with carnal inclinations: KJV - soldier, (go to) war (-fare).
[xix] Biblesoft's New Exhaustive Strong's Numbers and Concordance with Expanded Greek-Hebrew Dictionary. Copyright © 1994, 2003, 2006 Biblesoft, Inc. and International Bible Translators, Inc. NT:4752 NT:4752 stratei/a strateia (strat-i'-ah); from NT:4754; military service, i.e. (figuratively) the apostolic career (as one of hardship and danger): KJV - warfare.
[xx] Ephesians 2:20, the Apostle Paul in Acts 17:10 and Silas, a prophet, in Acts 15:32
[xxi] Revelation 1:6, Revelation 5:10
[xxii] Matthew 4:17, Matthew 24:14, and Mark 1:14

xxiii Biblesoft's New Exhaustive Strong's Numbers and Concordance with Expanded Greek-Hebrew Dictionary. Copyright © 1994, 2003, 2006 Biblesoft, Inc. and International Bible Translators, Inc. OT:2428 ly!j^ chayil (khah'-yil); from OT:2342; probably a force, whether of men, means or other resources; an army, wealth, virtue, valor, strength: KJV - able, activity, (+)army, band of men (soldiers), company, (great) forces, goods, host, might, power, riches, strength, strong, substance, train, (+)valiant (-ly), valour, virtuous (-ly), war, worthy (-ily).

xxiv 1 Corinthians 13:3

Wisdom for Building and War – Councils

xxv Proverbs 4:7
xxvi Proverbs 2:6
xxvii Proverbs 1:5
xxviii Proverbs 24:3-6

The Principle of Objective

xxix Proverbs 11:14
xxx Matthew 11:12
xxxi James 2:18, 26
xxxii http://www.generalpatton.com/quotes.html

The Principle of Mass

xxxiii Ephesians 4:11, 2 Corinthians 10:3-4, Ephesians 2:20, and 1 Corinthians 12:28
xxxiv 2 Timothy 1:8, Ephesians 6:10
xxxv Ephesians 6:10-11, 1 Corinthians 12 and Romans 12
xxxvi Matthew 28:19
xxxvii Leviticus 26:8, Deuteronomy 30:32
xxxviii Judges 7 – 8:21
xxxix Romans 12:1-2
xl (Biblesoft's New Exhaustive Strong's Numbers and Concordance with Expanded Greek-Hebrew Dictionary. Copyright © 1994, 2003, 2006 Biblesoft, Inc. and International Bible Translators, Inc.) NT:2842 NT:2842 koinwni/a koinonia (koy-nohn-ee'-ah); from NT: 2844; partnership, i.e. (literally) participation, or (social) intercourse, or (pecuniary) benefaction: KJV - (to) communicate (-ation), communion, (contri-) distribution, fellowship.

Principle of Mobility

xli Numbers 2:17
xlii Matthew 18:19
xliii Judges 6-8

Principle of Simplicity

[xliv] Numbers 31:14, Deuteronomy 20:9, and 1 Samuel 8:12
[xlv] Matthew 28:18
[xlvi] Acts 17:26

Principle of Security

[xlvii] 1 Corinthians 16:13, NIV
[xlviii] 1 Peter 5:8-11 , NKJV

Jesus and the Principles

[xlix] Hebrews 2:10, Joshua 5:15, Jude 14, and Revelation 19:1-16

Wisdom Applies the Principles

[l] 1 Timothy 1:8
[li] James 2:18-26
[lii] Hebrews 4:1
[liii] Acts 15:16-17, Amos 9:11-14, 2 Samuel 5:7, 1 Chronicles 13-16, and Psalm 18:6-14
[liv] Joel 2:1-10, Ezekiel 37:1-10, 1 Chronicles 11:1-3, Proverbs 31:23, Proverbs 9:1, and Isaiah 11:2
[lv] Isaiah 2:2-4, Micah 4:1-2
[lvi] Deuteronomy 32:30, Leviticus 26:8

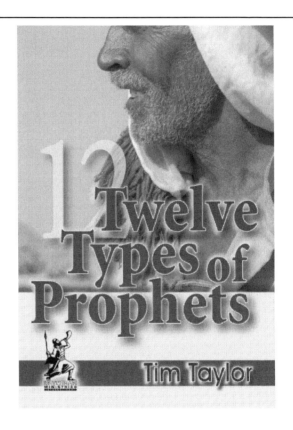

Order this insightful CD on www.KingdomLeague.org

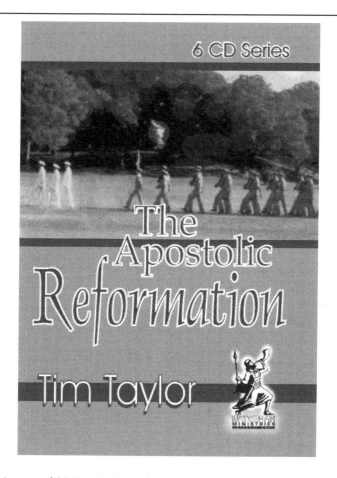

This is a powerful 6 CD series that looks at the 5 fold ministry based on Ephesians 4, and the Romans 12 and 1 Corinthian's 12 gifts in light of the current apostolic reformation. Learn how God is using these gift mixes in the church, business, government, media, education, healthcare and the family to transform society through everyday ordinary people with an extraordinary God. Order yours at www.KingdomLeague.org

This is the Operation Rolling Thunder Kit. It contains 4 hours of teaching CDs, a data CD and an amazing DVD highlighting the history, documented signs and wonders, and the measurable results seen in ORT. This is a companion to the Operation Rolling Thunder II book which equips leaders with all the tools needed to host a Kick Off for Operation Rolling Thunder in their communities.

www.KingdomLeague.org

Kingdom League International

4004 NE 4th Street, Suite 107-350

Renton, WA 98056

(425) 687-0994

www.KingdomLeague.org